T0266686

« MINECRAFT »
FARMING

UNOFFICIAL GAMER GUIDE

Zelda Wagner

Lerner Publications ◆ Minneapolis

Lerner Publications Company
An imprint of Lerner Publishing Group, Inc.
241 First Avenue North
Minneapolis, MN 55401 USA

For reading levels and more information, look up this title at www.lernerbooks.com.

Main body text set in ITC Franklin Gothic Std.
Typeface provided by Adobe Systems.

Editor: Cole Nelson **Designer:** Mary Ross **Photo Editor:** Angel Kidd
Lerner team: Martha Kranes

Library of Congress Cataloging-in-Publication Data

Names: Wagner, Zelda, 2000– author.
Title: Minecraft farming : unofficial gamer guide / Zelda Wagner.
Description: Minneapolis, MN : Lerner Publications, [2025] | Series: Updog books. Minecraft zone | Includes bibliographical references and index. | Audience: Ages 8–11 | Audience: Grades 2–3 | Summary: "In Minecraft, you can farm anything from pumpkins to potatoes. Whether they want to raise animals or grow crops, Minecraft players will learn how to farm like a pro"— Provided by publisher.
Identifiers: LCCN 2023040437 (print) | LCCN 2023040438 (ebook) | ISBN 9798765626504 (library binding) | ISBN 9798765629048 (paperback) | ISBN 9798765635483 (epub)
Subjects: LCSH: Minecraft (Game)—Juvenile literature. | Agriculture—Juvenile literature.
Classification: LCC GV1469.35.M535 W3423 2025 (print) | LCC GV1469.35.M535 (ebook) | DDC 794.8/5—dc23/eng/20231004

LC record available at https://lccn.loc.gov/2023040437
LC ebook record available at https://lccn.loc.gov/2023040438

Manufactured in the United States of America
1-1010171-51984-11/9/2023

TABLE OF CONTENTS

SURVIVING

To survive in *Minecraft*, you need to mine and explore.

You also need to grow
food. This is called farming.

A *Minecraft* farm can have plants and animals. Farm animals are livestock.

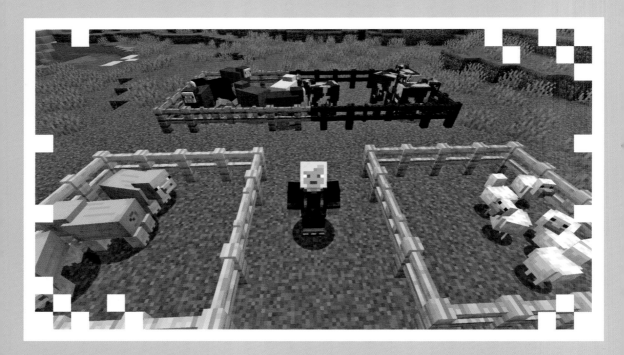

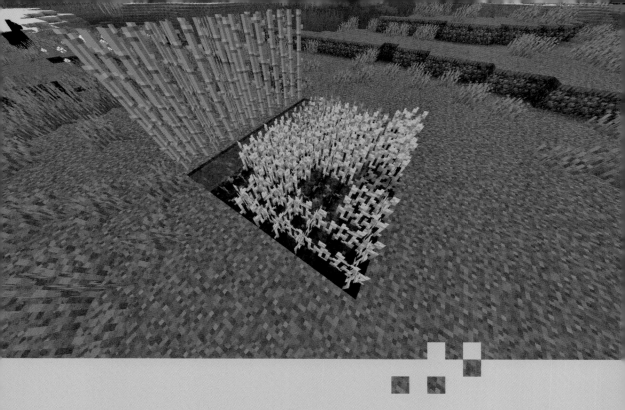

Plants grown on
a farm are crops.

Crops and livestock can
be turned into food.

≪ UP NEXT! ≫

GROWING CROPS AND
LIVESTOCK.

PLANTS AND ANIMALS

Your *Minecraft* farm can grow many kinds of foods!

You can farm vegetables
to fill your hunger bar.

You can grow wheat for crafting bread and feeding animals.

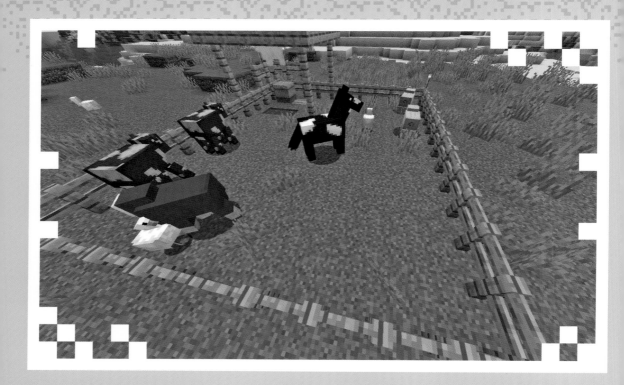

You can also farm chickens, sheep, cows, horses, and pigs.

Items from plants and animals
can be mixed to make other
foods, such as pumpkin pie.

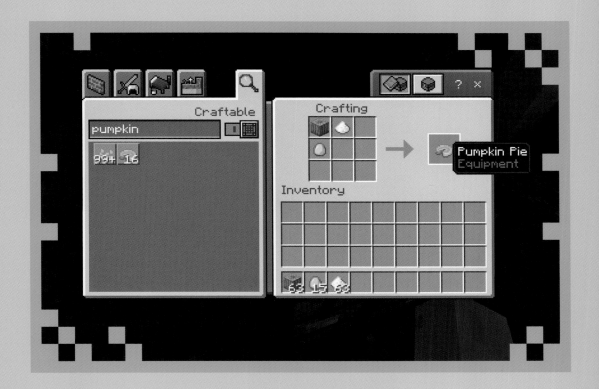

« GAME » BREAK!

Try farming these crops on your *Minecraft* farm:

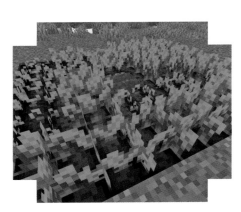

1.   Wheat

2.   Carrots

3.   Potatoes

4.   Apples

5.   Sugar cane

« **UP NEXT!** »

BUILDING YOUR FARM.

STARTING YOUR FARM

To get started, your farm needs grass, dirt, seeds, and water.

You can build your
farm outside, inside,
or even underground.

Garden Hoe   Shovel   Water Bucket   Shears

You can craft tools
to help you farm.

A garden hoe lets you plant seeds in dirt.

Shears gather wool from sheep.
Buckets carry water to plants.

« UP NEXT! »

PROTECTING YOUR FARM.

STAYING SAFE

Mobs show up at night and in the dark.

Torches make light that keeps mobs away from your farm.

Some crops, such as mushrooms, grow best in the dark.

Look out! If you don't light up the area, mobs may appear.

Place torches carefully
to keep mobs away.

《 UP NEXT! 》

REDSTONE FARM MACHINES.

FaRM MaCHINES

Just as in real life, some farmers in *Minecraft* use machines to make farming easier.

You can use redstone to power
machines, such as pistons.

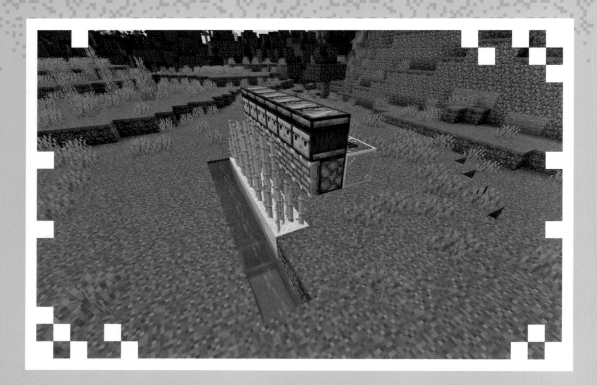

Pistons can harvest crops
when you are away.

There's so much you can grow on a *Minecraft* farm!

Glossary

crop: a plant grown by farmers

farm: a piece of land for growing crops or raising livestock

livestock: farm animals kept, raised, and used by people

mob: a creature in *Minecraft*. Hostile mobs attack players.

piston: an item that can move blocks, players, and monsters in front of it when powered

redstone: a *Minecraft* material used to power and program machines

Check It Out!

Kiddle: Farm Facts for Kids
https://kids.kiddle.co/Farm

Minecraft: A Beginner's Guide To Farming In *Minecraft*
https://help.minecraft.net/hc/en-us/articles
/360046311411-Minecraft-Farming-101

Minecraft Official Site
https://minecraft.net/en-us

Morison, S. D. *Your Unofficial Guide to Building Cool* Minecraft *Farms*. New York: Enslow, 2023.

Pang, Ursula. *Dairy Farms*. New York: PowerKids, 2023.

Wagner, Zelda. Minecraft *Survival Mode: Unofficial Gamer Guide*. Minneapolis: Lerner Publications, 2025.

Index

Photo Acknowledgments

Image credits: Various screenshots by Angel Kidd, Heather Schwartz, Julia Zajac, and Linda Zajac.

Other images: Phynart Studio/Getty Images, p.26. Design elements: Anatolii Poliashenko/Getty Images; filo/Getty Images.